RATIONAL APPROACH FOR MIDDLE MANAGERS

Learn from Others' Experiences

By

Rajiva Sharma

INDIA • SINGAPORE • MALAYSIA

Notion Press

Old No. 38, New No. 6
McNichols Road, Chetpet
Chennai - 600 031

First Published by Notion Press 2018
Copyright © Rajiva Sharma 2018
All Rights Reserved.

ISBN 978-1-64249-755-7

This book has been published with all reasonable efforts taken to make the material error-free after the consent of the author. No part of this book shall be used, reproduced in any manner whatsoever without written permission from the author, except in the case of brief quotations embodied in critical articles and reviews.

The Author of this book is solely responsible and liable for its content including but not limited to the views, representations, descriptions, statements, information, opinions and references ["Content"]. The Content of this book shall not constitute or be construed or deemed to reflect the opinion or expression of the Publisher or Editor. Neither the Publisher nor Editor endorse or approve the Content of this book or guarantee the reliability, accuracy or completeness of the Content published herein and do not make any representations or warranties of any kind, express or implied, including but not limited to the implied warranties of merchantability, fitness for a particular purpose. The Publisher and Editor shall not be liable whatsoever for any errors, omissions, whether such errors or omissions result from negligence, accident, or any other cause or claims for loss or damages of any kind, including without limitation, indirect or consequential loss or damage arising out of use, inability to use, or about the reliability, accuracy or sufficiency of the information contained in this book.

To

my wife, Rashmi, who edited the complete script alongside me as I progressed in writing.

Contents

Introduction		1
Chapter 1:	Learn to be Happy	3
Chapter 2:	Backup Plan	9
Chapter 3:	Lead by Personal Example	11
Chapter 4:	Dogged Determination	13
Chapter 5:	Work – Life Balance	17
Chapter 6:	Boss Management	21
Chapter 7:	Handling of Human Resources	27
Chapter 8:	Best Practices	35
Chapter 9:	Flexible Planning	39
Chapter 10:	Business Continuity Management	43
Chapter 11:	Acknowledgement of Communication	45
Chapter 12:	Accept Challenges and Take Calculated Risks	47
Chapter 13:	Temper Is Valuable Don't Lose It but Manage Anger	49
Chapter 14:	Offence and Punishment	55
Chapter 15:	Training and Change Management	57

Chapter 16:	Terms of Reference (ToR) of the Jobs and Standard Operating Procedures (SOP)	59
Chapter 17:	Under Cutting and Cockroach/Crab Mentality	61
Chapter 18:	Variety of People in Organization	63
Chapter 19:	Participative Management (Quality Circles)	65
Chapter 20:	Delegation and Empowerment	67
Chapter 21:	Circulate Grapevine Before Passing Sensitive Orders	69
Chapter 22:	Extra Marital Relations or Stealing the Affection of Colleague's Spouse	71
Chapter 23:	Avoid Roadside Brawls	73
Chapter 24:	Eye for Details	75
Chapter 25:	Self Grooming and Etiquettes	77
Chapter 26:	Social Activities	79
Chapter 27:	Not Getting Along in Joint Families	83
Chapter 28:	Sacking an Engineer on Dishonesty	85
Chapter 29:	Punishment Reforms	87
Chapter 30:	Never Promote Incompetent Person	89
Chapter 31:	Provide Necessary Facilities	91
Chapter 32:	Regularize the Actions Beyond Control	93
Chapter 33:	Determination of Joining Army and United Nations	95
Chapter 34:	Remain Cool in Crisis	97
Chapter 35:	Aiming for Perfection	99

Conclusion — *101*

Introduction

After my earlier books "Eye for Details – Prepare to Join Corporate World (Published by Partridge India) and Rational Thinking for Winners (Published by Notion Press)" concentrating on the problems of beginners, I got motivated to write my mind for middle managers too.

Freshers do graduate to the level of middle managers. This means that they have to manage a team under them and shoulder additional responsibilities. Middle managers maintain a central position in organizational hierarchies, are responsible for implementing senior management strategies, and exercise control over junior staff. They also become an important part of planning and execution of projects the sizes of which will depend on their experience and capabilities. Their problems will be different compared to those of the green horns and accountability will be more. Thus they will have more powers and improved remunerations. They will be required to handle more stress both at work place and also in domestic life. Children will be growing and their demands will be increasing. Even if the parents are not dependant on middle managers but they would have the concern about their well being. It is expected that the Middle Managers would have overcome *seven years itch* after marriage and they would have crossed over differences with their spouse and accepted the relationship as it is.

The topics covered in this book may already be known to you but I have attempted to consolidate them at one place as an 'Aide de Memoire' where one should focus. It will be a herculean task to include all possible ones in this small book but exposures to these ones will orient readers to select areas of their concerns and develop them as own time work. This book I have written suggesting the readers how to prepare themselves for middle level management phase of career/life. Like in my earlier book the writing is simple to read and is divided into two parts. One – how to prepare to face the different scenario and in part two the actual cases studies which I handled.

Chapter 1
Learn to be Happy

Although whether to remain happy or not, is an individual's psychological state of mind but it is possible to change it to a positive mind set if a conscious effort is made in this direction. It is very easy to remain unhappy on small things but it requires versatile thought process to remain happy under all circumstances. I don't mean to say that even if there is a tragedy in front of you still you keep laughing or smiling. Happiness to my understanding is the relaxed and peaceful state of mind. In such conditions you remain balanced and you think rationally.

At middle managerial level since you are the buffer between the senior managers and workers, you are sandwiched between the pressure from the top and resistance from the bottom. So you have no option but to remain physically and mentally robust to absorb both the pressures and keep smiling. To achieve this state of mind a mastery over "Prioritization" and "Time Management" are the keys to success.

It is not possible to list out all the points and actions which will keep you happy and confident but some common salient ones are listed below:

a) Have trust in the power of nature or God almighty. My experience says that when in crisis even the most atheist person remembers the super natural power. Although he/she may not confess publicly but this action gives them some strength to fight out the situation.

b) You are responsible for your own health. A good health will keep you mentally and physically robust, tough in handling the day today problems. In order to achieve it, regular exercises and healthy food on time are the best things to follow. There is no requirement to join a gymnasium if you can do about 30 minutes of walk five days in a week. I used to do the same. It has two advantages. One – it revamps and revitalizes the body and two – it reduces the stress, stimulates your thinking and thus you can find the solutions of the problems you slept with in the night. I found it very useful.

c) Never miss your main three meals. Take it on time and don't depend on junk food for lack of time as a practice or to reduce the weight. Feasting and fasting both are the causes of weight gains.

d) There is an old saying *Procrastination is the thief of time*. If you shelve actions or put a problem under the carpet, it may be possible that they get bloated out of proportion over the passage of time and later you have to invest more time and funds to resolve the same at the cost of unbudgeted expenses. Therefore, it is advisable to immediately handle the situation by *taking the bull by its horns*. This way you will not carry forward the burden of back log

and will remain light always. It is better to make a note of *To Do List* and keep reviewing it.
e) Draping in comfortable and impressive clothes will increase your self confidence. View yourself in the mirror after getting ready to go out. This gives you feeling of happiness. Get dressed as per the occasion and which suites your age and social status. Wearing torn jeans and a faded tee shirt is apt for film industry but for the formal financial investment meet an elegant business suite is more appreciated. Walk smartly, talk gracefully and conduct elegantly.
f) Your computer should have your favorite information like memories, pictures of close ones, requisite profession data, movies, your preferred music etc.
g) Plan and control your finances so that there is always requisite liquidity available to face the unexpected eventualities. In the same category I recommend you to have adequate insurance covers for life, medical emergencies and house hold items including expensive jewelry.
h) Plan your family outings regularly and visit the places which are different from the ones you have already seen. Take the advantage of the opportunity where you can combine the official trip with pleasure if possible.
i) Spend personal funds in collecting new gadgets, useful books, music etc to enhance your general knowledge and also enhancement of professional/ personal skills.

j) Mix up with team freely and understand them well without compromising the level of frankness and maintaining the distance.

k) Maintain highest quality of conduct in everything what you perform. Remember *Quality is Free*.

l) In nut shell, do the self analysis on SWOT (**S**trengths, **W**eaknesses, **O**pportunities and **T**hreats) pattern and address your short comings in advance so that they don't become the causes of your unhappiness in life.

m) Most of us are a victim of fear of unknown. These fears are the main causes of retarding factors for success in life. And fears are nowhere but in our minds. If we can control this situation by developing more and more self confidence, no one on this earth can stop us from being happy.

n) Accept that the *life* is a struggle at all levels and ages. If there is *life* there is struggle. Master the struggle craft and be successful. If you stop struggling you don't lead a good *life*.

o) Punctuality should be part of your personality. Imagine you call your staff for a meeting and all of them come on time except you because you are the boss and cannot be pointed out by any one. I calculate the loss like:

   i) No. of staff members called for meeting = 5
   ii) You are late by = 15 minutes
   iii) Per hour average salary per person = $50
   iv) Straight loss = $5 x 50 x 15/60 $62.50
   v) 5 employees could have utilized 15 minutes = $62.5 x 2 = $125

vi) Thus the net loss to organization will be $125.

You are not punctual if you don't manage your time well. There are many reasons which could be attributed to this bad habit of poor planning which exhibits no respect for others' time.

p) Be polite and firm. Never raise your voice during conversation. It sounds like quarrel and draws attention of all working around. Employees who are shouted upon hate it because it is insulting to them. Imagine how you would feel if you are in their place? It is equally applicable at home when you are with family. Believe in following:

Never fight with a pig, both will get dirty and pig will enjoy it.

q) Locate and earmark a most accessible multi specialty medical facility close to your residence for the complete family.

r) Select a residence which is most conveniently located for all of you.

s) It is a good practice to clear your routine payments as soon as you receive the bills. If you procrastinate them you may either forget it or run at the eleventh hour to do so.

t) Don't read only success stories, they give you good feelings and a message while if you read about the failures you have a choice to exercise your brain too. Give compliments freely. It makes you feel relaxed.

u) Bargaining for petty amounts with roadside vendor (specially the vegetable hawker) or at Car Parking should be considered as an act below your dignity. You never do it in The Malls so why do it with poor man?

v) Never be egoist as ego is inversely proportionate to knowledge. Persons with less knowledge are more egoists and vice versa. It is advisable to drop the ego because it breaks the relationship and you are isolated.

w) Be bold to fight the situation out when you lose and be humble and calm when you win.

x) Do what makes you happy as you are responsible for your happiness.

Chapter 2
Backup Plan

We are living in an uncertain world. What happens tomorrow is not known. In this situation, it is important that for all our responsibilities, we should have a big or small backup plan. This plan should be for both your professional life and domestic life. For example, you are working in an organization, and suddenly, you have to leave because of any reason. Do you have enough savings to sustain yourself till you get another assignment, or are your parents rich enough to support you? Tomorrow, there is a medical emergency, and you are not covered by the organization's medical insurance, then how will you cope up with the medical expenses? Irrespective of medical insurance coverage from the employer, I always have one of my own. It is important to cover the period when you are out of job, which may happen any time in life. I have heard many people say "Oh, the journey was too long and I got bored" or "I had to wait for such a long time that it was so boring." We all have such situations one time or another. I've also had them, but to overcome the boredom, I keep thinking about the backup plans.

I make my own situations possible—in the office or at home—and try to find the solution. If you also do the same, you will never be in a dilemma and feel lost when suddenly you are in a thick soup because you have already planned how to swim out. This planning activity gives you self-confidence in your life and you exhibit a cool temperament in the society. Many a times in our lives, we delegate a job to someone based on our confidence in him/her and the capability of the individual. We also give the target date and time to complete the job. And then at the eleventh hour, when you ask about the result/the output, the individual pulls up a blank face with a flimsy excuse in front of you and says, "Sir, I got stuck somewhere or another and could not complete the job." You feel like pulling your hairs and punching him/her on the nose because based on his/her output, you have to build up further. To overcome this phenomenon, I do two things. One, there is a small display on my table where 'No surprises, please' is written; another one is periodical stage inspections. The result is that all my junior colleagues, whenever they visit my office, would see the display and get reminded of not giving me a surprise-a psychological warfare-and carrying out the stage inspections would give me confidence that the work in progress is moving in the right direction and pace. So, no tension for me.

Chapter 3
Lead by Personal Example

To become an effective leader it is most important to know what are the qualities needed to lead a particular business. The factors needed to know are the work culture of the organization, the type of business, responses of superior team in general and the top leader in particular, the social/industrial environment around the location etc. After knowing fully about the work place, evaluate how you will fit in the system and changes you have to fine tune to be the leader?

In any field of activity you are a leader even if you have one person reporting to you. That means minimum two eyes are always looking towards you for guidance and help – may be at work place or while encountering the personal problems also. You are under watch and hence you have to set personal example of good code of conduct and have a positive attitude. As you grow up the No. of eyes looking at you keep increasing and any good or bad deed of yours spreads in the organization at a very fast pace.

At junior level you are known in your organization but as you grow up you are known in the industry at national level and later globally. Therefore, there should be total excellence in your attitude, conduct and behavior. Remember you are being watched every moment – the way you walk, dress, talk, react, handle the crisis, communicate with superiors, team players, outside agencies, customers even your eating habits etc. It is very commonly said, "Our Manager leads from front." A leader who is executing the plan has to be in the front. Anybody who stays behind is not a leader but a follower.

Chapter 4
Dogged Determination

I have experienced that determination to achieve a decided goal is always challenging task. Things in day today life are not easy to handle. You have obstructions everywhere. If other things are fine your peers, seniors or juniors will try their best to let you down. Don't get deterred, keep trying and you will find clouds clearing in front of you. Remember the story of deaf and dumb frog who reached at the top of a hill because he couldn't hear what other participants of the race were talking and being dumb he couldn't participate in idle gossips. He maintained the focus and kept climbing up to win the race. I accept the challenges and then plan how to accomplish them. This keeps me flexible in approach. If you plan certain project in a rigid manner and don't see it progressing as per plan, then you have to undo the plan and do it a fresh. This is frustrating. So keep your plans flexible and also keep Plan B as standby.

Once for some period I was without any regular assignment. I had decided to focus on international opportunities with fat pay packages. It was tough decision. But I believe in a common saying that if you strongly "will," for a goal with full determination, all the cosmic powers of universe get together to support you to ensure that you achieve what you have endeavored to get. This belief, I have drawn from the hymns by Guru Gobind Singh, the tenth Sikh Guru:

Deh siva bar mohe eh-hey subh karman te kabhu na taro
*Na daro arr seo jab jaye laro **nischey kar apni jit karo.***
Arr Sikh ho apne he mann ko, eh laalach hou gun tau ucharo.
Jab aav ki audh nidan bane att he rann me tabh joojh maro.

Translation:

Dear God, grant my request so that I may never deviate from doing good deeds
That, I shall have no fear of the enemy when **I go into battle and with determination I will be victorious**
That, I may teach my mind to only sing your praises
And when the time comes, I should die fighting heroically on the field of battle

My interpretation of above is that first I fix the goal and then I make plans and win. Attempting anything without am aim is like firing in the air and wasting of time, money and energy. Money you can recover later from elsewhere but lost time and energy are irrecoverable. Losing of time is also linked to aging which results into losing of energy.

Basically you have got to believe in yourself then you will be able to achieve. Never laugh on others failures. If you doubt your caliber you see a mountain of problems in front of you but if you are confident you can see the flattening of mountains. Only weak persons seek sympathies. Achievers appreciate liberally and take the total responsibilities of their deeds and weak persons try to blame others or pass the buck to others' shoulders. If you are under performing a task don't hesitate in accepting it. Only if you work you are likely to commit mistakes because no one is perfect. More important is how fast you can resolve the problem and come back on the right track.

Chapter 5
Work – Life Balance

Work, work, work, and no recreation or respite. Many of us feel that if we work for extended hours, day in and day out, we are the star performers. Well your boss will always say so. Our brain and body have certain limitations. If we consistently stretch them more than their elastic limits, they will stop working or slow down. That is probably why the labor law has been made for eight working hours a day. I have observed when people are made to work continuously for more than these working hours, their efficiency drops to 50 per cent.

So after eight hours, you get 50 per cent output and you pay double the overtime allowance. Therefore, getting overtime for a protracted period is not economical. Yes, randomly, to meet certain targets, there is no harm going to overtime work. We all have families. When you are not married and are staying with your parents or alone, you come and go any time, and no one objects, except that your mother gets up even in the late hours to serve you hot food when you come home. But when you are married, you have to take out time to be together with your family. Don't forget that this time will never return. So plan your schedule in such a manner that you spend some quality time which is highly recreational with your spouse and children. There is this saying:

When I was young, I had time and energy but no money.
When I was middle-aged, I had energy but no time and money.
Now I am old, I have time and money but no energy.

If you feel that you are unable to leave the office on time, then either you are inefficient or you waste your time in idle gossips during working hours or you are trying to bite more than what you can chew. Lastly, there is shortage of workforce in your department. For all these you have to take appropriate actions.

Regular exercise not only keeps you physically fit but is also a means of recreation. I've found going for a walk early in the morning is the best physical-fitness activity. It requires only a pair of comfortable shoes. I have gotten solutions to many a problem only during my morning walks. In your future planning never procrastinate in any of the activities, linking one with another. For example: "I will do this particular thing when this thing will happen." There is a famous saying that goes like this:

*First, I was **dying** to finish high school and start college,*
*and then I was **dying** to finish college and start working.*
*Then I was **dying** to get married and have family.*
*And then I was **dying** to get my kids settled. I was then too much tired*
*of working and was **dying** to retire and relax. And now I am actually frail, and I am **dying** to **die**. Lastly, when I look back,*

*I realize that time has flown, life has been very short, I had been **dying** only and I've forgotten to **live** the way I wanted.*

When you forget to live and realize that you have forgotten, you get frustrated, and your health starts deteriorating faster than normal.

To sum up, we require quality time with family every day, family holiday, some routine physical exercises, recreation and all this is possible only with excellent time management.

Chapter 6
Boss Management

Smartly managing the bosses is an important skill in the managers. Boss doesn't only mean the person you are reporting to in the hierarchy of the organization. I believe anybody who is your *customer* is your boss. Otherwise as per Compact Oxford Dictionary, boss is a person who is in charge of an employee/organization. Another meaning is boss is a person who give orders in domineering manner.

But in my experience I have seen three types of bosses. One who are always dictatorial and think that what they say, are orders, and orders are laws (unchallengeable). These people always wore tense looks and found an opportunity to criticize your work. Most of these types are shallow in knowledge, lacking confidence and invariably are scared of failures. Without being competent they try to achieve fail safe approach and don't hesitate in blaming others for any mistakes. This act of passing the buck is also termed as CMA (Cover My Ass). They are always scared of their superiors in the office, their customers and with their wives at home. I handled one of such bosses. If you are professionally sound and boss is convinced that you are indispensible, your boss will never bully you. I never used to open all my cards in front of him and thus made him fully dependent on me. Also if he used to behave dictatorially I used to tell him the correct picture and get his written approval on his orders. If the boss signed then they are his/her orders. If he/she used to refuse to sign I used to make minutes of discussions – my points and his final decision over ruling my suggestions and keep a record in office before releasing the orders. Later while in the lighter moments I used to narrate the stories of some incident where such wrong decisions were taken and the boss had to suffer. Normally weak shouting bosses get scared. If you go to them with a problem their reaction will be, "Go do it yourself. You are paid for this. Whenever you come with problem you should bring three solutions also." Most of them are never happy with anything you do. They will try to find mistakes in your work and then start bullying. I call them weeping managers.

I came across one such boss. He had problem with my English. Whenever I used to send a draft long letter for his approval, he used to return the same to me with remarks like, "Poor English" or "Atrocious English" etc. He had done his schooling from an English school in Delhi. When I got fed up of such remarks I walked in his office and told him that I am from a Government School and simple English what I write is for common understanding and for Oxford Graduates. He took it with a pinch of salt and gave a disapproving looks. I was waiting for another opportunity to corner him which came very fast. He was proceeding on a twenty days leave. Before proceeding he gave me a hand written draft policy letter with instructions to finalize the same and put up to him on his return from leave for his signatures. I got the final letter made and got it put up to him under my initials. He saw it and sent the letter back to me with remarks, "Stupid English." I got the opportunity. I took the final, mechanical typewriter written letter along with his hand written one and asked him the reason for remark. He saw his remark and said, "Yes it is stupid English." I replied, "Chief this is not my English. This is the typewriter written copy of your hand written draft." He got cheesed off. He looked at me through his powered glasses resting at the tip of his nose, adjusted his big moustache, lit a cigarette and told me, "Get lost."

After this incident his remarks on my English got buried. He is retired now. When he meets me in the Club or on the roadside, knowing that my books have global fan following, he keeps asking me, "Rajiva, when is your next book being published? Keep a copy reserved for me."

Second types of bosses are leaders. They pull you out of the crisis. For them credit of success is for the team while they own the responsibly if the team doesn't succeed. They remain in good mood and are confident of resolving your problems. If they don't know the answer they will accept the ignorance and make you part of their team and look around for the solution. They are, "Let's do it," type superior manager. You can call them *"super-wisers"* too. I like such leaders and also behave the same way with my team. My instructions to my team members used to be to help each other as much as they could but within the framework of rules. This helped me in having excellent interpersonal relations.

Third type of boss I came across was always smiling and laughing. While dealing with us the stronger he will laugh more harm he will cause to you. He never used to shout or show gestures of disgust but immediately issue a memo asking explanations in writing and keep a record of these actions in employees' performance dossier. He was the most unpredicted back stabber. In those good old days there was no system of discussing the performance reports. A staff member would come to know only when he was overlooked for promotion. Best way to survive with these bosses is to keep away from them.

Customer is also your boss and should be given all importance. First of all listen to his/her requirements very carefully and patiently. God has given us two ears and one mouth. So use them in the ratio of 2:1. Try to give them a simpler and cost effective solution for his/her product and realistic time frame to make them feel thrilled. Understand his/her urgency and inform the customer with reasons if you cannot stick to their time schedule. All conversation should be recorded and mutually agreed before putting the signatures. After the sign off keep in continuous touch, so that mutual confidence is maintained. If required it will be good practice to get a stage inspection of quality done by the customer. While doing so, NEVER GIVE SURPRISES, of non performance, on the delivery date.

Customers will be happy to receive the product as per their specifications because they have planned further accordingly. For example, a car is a car but there is lots of difference between 800 cc or 3.5 L cars. Also never try to give Indian villager chocolates to eat if they like sweet meat.

Therefore, the definition of Best Quality is to adhere to the "customers' specifications."

Along with the learning the dynamics of Boss Management the most important is to understand thoroughly his expectations and ego. Plan your smart strategy to keep the boss comfortable and don't ever irritate him. Win – win situation rather than locking horn is good for both.

Chapter 7
Handling of Human Resources

Once during my lean period I was running my own business of HR Recruitment Consultancy for IT Professionals and CEOs. Since the industry was new, the promoters although had the funds to invest but were not familiar with the conduct and behavior of the new computer trained kids who used to adopt the *Yankee* culture after their returns from post orientation visit to USA. They used to address their superiors by first names and used to raise too many observations everywhere.

The promoter appointed a technically well qualified CEO who had about ten years of experience in IT Industry. Handling of manpower is one of the most difficult tasks and requires more experience than qualifications. One day the CEO called me up and said, "Sir, you know mine is a startup IT Company. My team members have got together and are refusing to work. I don't know how to handle them? If the promoter comes to know he will fire me from the job. Please leave all your work and drive down to my office to control the employees." I understood the problem. On reaching the location I spoke to the employees. The problem turned out to be the same which I had anticipated. These youngsters told me that they are not guided properly about what they are supposed to do and are kept in dark about theirs and company's future plans. CEO never used to communicate with them. On further discussion I noticed that there were no systems in the organization. The reason was that the CEO was not experienced on how to raise a new organization and make the foolproof systems. He was qualified in technology but was clueless about the administration and human resource management. I made him understand the ways how to go about and how he should conduct while dealing with his team. It took a couple of days but the company came on track.

Human brain may design the automation but to implement the same the requirement of human being cannot be dispensed with. Even in the ultimate situation of automation in any organization there will be a team of human beings working. Since the top management would insist on slimmest establishment all the workers are bound to be super experts in their fields and will have inherent problem of not understanding or low understanding of other section's working. This will lead to frequent differences among them causing gaps in inter personnel relations and split teams. This could lead to a bad work culture and visible tense atmosphere in the organizations. Thus affecting, adversely, the efficiency of the product output and poor impression of the organization among the customers. While I am writing this in early months of year 2018 the writing on the wall is clear about the future.

During my days in the lead roles in managing the organizations I have successfully tried to focus on certain areas which are listed below.

a) **Try to Remember the First Names of all Your Team Members:** If the team is big it is not easy but try to do it as much as you can. There is no harm in finding out the names before meeting the individuals. Addressing someone by their first names creates immediate bonding and the person feels important.

b) **Pleasant Disposition:** Having a pleasing disposition with full control over anger is very important and makes you popular anywhere in the society. Nobody likes persons with growling looks and thus are ignored as they transmit bad vibes. You smile, everyone will smile with you and the atmosphere will have nice fragrance of softness.

c) **Awareness of Personal Problems:** Be aware of your team mates' domestic and personal problems also because this has direct bearing on their performances.

d) **Clarity of Planning and Implementation:** Planning is the first stage of a project. Accurate and realistic planning makes the foundation of the operations strong enough to make a reliable superstructure of the project. The planners should make achievable and economically viable plan which is not complicated. It could be easily understood and implemented by the operations team. Before clearing for implementation the team members should be given time to study the plan and have group discussions. All suggestions should be evaluated in a positive way and not brushed aside. The questions should be answered clearly leaving no doubts in the language which is understood by all.

e) **Operations:** The organizations are continuously in either planning modes or operations mode. There are separate teams deployed for these actions.

f) **Information Sharing:** In any organization various types of information keep flowing in the air. Some are written while others are verbal. Since verbal are not supported by any proof they can be labeled as gossip or even grapevine. The human nature is to spread these as much as possible. Remember the game," Chinese whisper" which is still being played in school. As soon as you come across such gossip especially which is wrong counter it and tell the team about the truth. However, you may take a decision and are not confident of its acceptance or correctness. In such circumstances it is very much in order to spread grapevine and very soon you will have general reaction of the team which will facilitate you to implement your decision successfully.

Information is to be shared very discretely and is done on, "Need to know basis" otherwise people who are not in full picture may misinterpret the same. I used to address all the employees every month to share the general happenings like in a "Town Hall Meeting" and in addition sometimes discretely with chosen staff with an intention to wipe off gossips among workers at all levels. In

Town Hall meeting employees were permitted to ask any questions of common interest.

In addition employees were routing their personal problems through the departmental channels but they were also allowed to meet me in my office.

g) **Raise the Flag before the Mistakes Occur:** Once on my routine round of the production floor I noticed one technician was following wrong procedure in the assembly area and his supervisor was watching very eagerly. I asked the supervisor, "Do you see this person is following a wrong procedure?" The supervisor smiled and replied promptly, "Yes Sir, I know but I am waiting to let him fully commit the mistake and then I will catch him and pull him up." I told him, "This is your sadistic approach and I take it against your way of working. Have you ever thought if I do the same thing with you, how will you feel? By doing this awkward act you are not only wasting production time but also creating tension in atmosphere." The supervisor felt small and apologized.

h) **Never Compare the Performances:** It is a wrong practice to compare the performances of two employees publicly. The contents of your conversation spread in organization like wild fire and thus disturbs the atmosphere at the work place. Beside this always give equal opportunity to the employees to prove their worth. Partial behavior of the leader de-motivates the team. Leaders have to hold the hands of weak team members and try to make them as strong as others. Don't forget that:

> *Team is like a chain. Strength of the chain is the strength of weakest link.*

i) **Encourage Non Performers to Improve:** There are good performers and there are bad performers in your team. You have to analyze the reasons of bad performances and facilitate to help the person. There could be many reasons including personal/domestic.

j) **Show the Brighter Side of Work:** While interacting (formally or informally) with the team members, it is better to discuss convincingly the brighter side of the work, skill development, their importance and future in the organization. Also the growth potential of the organization in the global market. This motivates the employees to take pride in their performance, with greater responsibilities and with enhanced loyalty.

k) **Appraisals:** Appraising the performance is tool to assist you for the pace of growth of employees. Although generally the best time to revise the promotion and package in the beginning of financial year but many of the organizations do it on the anniversary of joining date. I believe in periodical assessment before the final appraisal. If you feel an employee under you is not living up to the expectations, he/she should be counseled and record should be kept in the dossier. If the person doesn't improve after verbal advises, then he/she should be put under Performance Improvement Plan (PIP) with quarterly assessment system which is discussed with the employee at every end of three months. At the time of annual appraisal the recordings of the PIP should be of major consideration for promotion and level of pay package. Thus the employee will be well aware in advance of what is expected in the annual appraisal. And also full justice has been done by the organization by giving them opportunity to improve the performance. I never sacked an employee without giving him adequate chance to improve. As a thumb rule if employee separates from the organization the financial loss is approximately equivalent to his/her one year package.

Chapter 8
Best Practices

Keep updating the best practices and follow them in your everyday routine so that you are always prepared to prevent or handle the worst situations.

The first best practice is to look after our health so that we are mentally and physically fit enough to take care of our responsibilities. When you have a healthy body you will have a healthy mind too. If that be so, you will be able to coup up with the day today stress and will remain cheerful with positive attitude. Competitions are everywhere in the life with new challenges. Do participate in the run. Get fully charged up with an aim to win but smartly by doing something different than what others are doing. You will stand apart. But I recommend:

Don't run a rat race. Even if you win you will be a rat only.

We know that commonly a rat is a rodent but as per Compact Oxford Dictionary rat also means *an unpleasant person*. With this meaning you can interpret the message in the above phrase when used in the corporate world. You have chosen your profession at your will therefore; enjoy what you do in life. Be inquisitive and don't feel shy in asking even basic questions. If you don't clarify your doubts you will remain in doubt which may hamper you planning. If as an afterthought, you feel you have chosen a wrong profession try to do an honest SWOT (**S**trength, **W**eakness, **O**pportunity and **T**hreat) Analysis. Try to change the course of actions in accordance of new considerations to have better job satisfactions. Course correction could be small but if required and you have confidence go for aggressive implementation of hard decisions. I took premature retirement at my will with 21 years of meritorious service in Indian Army and plunged into absolutely new culture of private sector. Every one among my friends and family advised me against the decision. At this stage like any other person I had growing up children and liability of financial loans. But my wife Rashmi supported me blindly for the same. My experience is that if your spouse is cooperating with you, than together you can take risks.

I searched the job in advance took a commitment from the new private employer and then processed my resignation. Initially I got less remuneration but adding them with my pension, I was at par with the managers with 21 years of service. I learnt the new procedures and smartly worked with common sense. In nine months I caught on to the package as per the ongoing industrial standards besides my pension. Rashmi and I had done very honest and detailed SWOT Analysis. I believe that we should never compare with anyone but do compete. Remember the story of deaf and dumb frog who, when was in a run to climb the hill reached first because he was concentrating on the goal while others were busy talking and wasting their time trying to find faults with competitors and idle gossips. Successful people have positive attitude, cheerful disposition, considerate and help others while unsuccessful persons have negative mind set and try to pull down others.

When you ascend in the corporate ladder even if you have one person reporting to you, you are a leader. Some people like to be called "Boss." Boss is different from leader. Boss orders and expect results without him being bothered while a leader helps you in correcting the course if you are going on a wrong track. As leader you have to develop the team under you. While doing so keep in mind the following good old proverb:

He who knows not and knows not that he knows not:
he is ignorant – update him.
He who knows not and knows he knows not: he is
simple – teach him.
He who knows and knows not he knows:
he is a sleep – wake him.
He who knows and knows he knows: he is wise – follow him.

To summarize the above, it is your responsibility to develop the persons under you and also how you develop yourself. Some people have been lucky to have succeeded with bad qualities, shoe shining of boss and following the malpractices also but they are very rare and get stagnated in the ladder of promotions. I have experienced that smart work is the combination of honest work and attitude. This only will take you to altitude.

The thumb rule is that under the guidance of the global best practices make a separate plan for your organization depending on your requirement, circumstances, working conditions, human behavior and environment before implementing them. A practice which is highly acceptable in Japan may not be yielding the same results in India. Why compare the two countries, I found in the same organization, three works located in the Punjab, Haryana and Goa in India had different culture and working conditions. Thus we had to make different implementation plan for the three locations.

Chapter 9
Flexible Planning

Planning is an ongoing process and should be done carefully with clearly defined goals. Life is busy because there is always shortage of time. At the end of the day many a times we realize that we missed out something which may result in some sort of disturbance in our minds. The causes could be personal or official but we have to bear the brunt. Ultimately we are the worst sufferer and we curse ourselves and say, "What the hell? I have been working so hard in office still I get kicked. I try to keep my family comfortable by trying to earn more but still I have to listen to sarcasm and some comparison with the success of family in neighborhood. What do I do? What additional can I do?"

Answer is simple. Write down your carrier plan on a paper or on your computer. The plan essentially should have two parts. Part 1 – Short Term Goals for five years and Part 2 – Long Term Goals which could be of 15 or 20 years. Getting ready to achieve both the goals you should make a plan based on your present qualifications, experience, commitments and the time available. Also the short term goal plan should have clear picture for actions required to be taken to prepare you to achieve the Long Term Goals.

However, the element of flexibility has to be in built in both the situations, because in today highly dynamic world you cannot foresee everything. Keep reviewing the anticipated threats on each mile stone you cross successfully. Visualize problems expected and keep an alternative plan ready for business continuity. This clarity is very necessary otherwise you will be running amok, aimlessly and directionless like headless chicken asking for help from whoever comes across you and become a laughing stock. For example you never go to the railway platform and board a train going in any direction. Never worry about the mistakes in life but have confidence in yourself to quickly analyze what went wrong, reconcile and move ahead to recover the losses.

Life is like road journey,
You have cross country drives, Water Bound Macadam (WBM) roads, and express ways too.
Whatever time you lose on rough roads you do make it up on express ways.

The first step to plan is to make a realistic and achievable TO DO list. Follow it with continuous fine tuning as and when required. This list should be made regularly with about 10% flexibility to cover unforeseen circumstances, so that there are no pending actions which are to be brought forward for the next day. To ensure that all planned actions have been taken you should be clear on PRIOROTIES and also how to demarcate between URGENT and IMPORTANT. An urgent action may not be important and the vice versa. *Important* actions are those which are necessary to achieve the goal in stipulated time frame while *Urgent* activities are to be attended forthwith and are associated with clients' requirement because if not attended on time they have immediate adverse effects on business.

To summarize, all plans should have the elements of simplicity and flexibility like the flow of fluids who take the shapes of easiest path of least resistance to destination. Simple plans are easy to explain, understand and implement.

Chapter 10
Business Continuity Management

Business Continuity Management (BCM) is to identify the potential threat which could hamper the routine business and to be ready with resources in advance to implement the plan for building resilience to recover the damaged system and make the business as usual in shortest possible time with minimum losses. This can also be termed as Substantive Backup Plan in simple language. I have BCM for my domestic life also.

I recommend every Section in the organization should have BCM Plan properly documented and explained to the concern persons. Further an integrated Plan for the organization be made to carry out a mock exercise at least two times in a year to assess the effectiveness of the same. I had been the author of Business Continuity Plan for United Nations Peace Keeping Mission and coordinated the mock drill for the same. It worked pretty well.

Long time ago in one of the production units, I discussed this with all the HoDs to informally try and see how the supervisors manage the show in the absence of the Managers. There was no formal BCM available. So I called a meeting of all the Managers and their next in command. I explained my idea of sending out of station the Managers for three days and two nights after handing over the responsibilities to next supervisors in command. Instructions to the senior most supervisors were that they will call us only if there is a fire in the factory or someone dies.

One or two HoDs expressed their lack of confidence in this act. I told them, "If you are not confident that means you have not worked on policy of preparing your subordinates for higher responsibilities." On hearing this they meekly agreed to the suggestion. The idea was to assess the level of resilience, self confidence and preparation of succession plan.

During my stay out of station, I didn't receive any phone call. That was an indication that all is generally well. On our return the supervisors of Production and Quality Assurance (QA) Sections informed that there was a problem in the design of product. It was not passing the stage QA tests. Supervisors got together studied the problem and found that there was a small design error. They found the solution and implemented the same after taking the approval of the customer. All this was done in record one working day. They also managed the production line in such a manner that there was no production loss. After this I was confident that the team is competent and well trained. This also injected additional amount of zeal in all the workers. Followed by this incident we made a proper BCM Plan and documented the same as per ISO standards. This could be quoted as an example of *delegation and empowerment.*

Chapter 11
Acknowledgement of Communication

Acknowledgement of receipt of information either verbal or written is the confirmation of clear understanding of the communication. Therefore, it gives satisfaction to both the sides that cycle is complete and there is no ambiguity.

Chapter 12
Accept Challenges and Take Calculated Risks

Life is all about taking risks. More the experience you have sharper and successful you are at the risky games. Once plunged into action, be positive, show determination, be guile based on situation, monitor progress closely with a magnifying lens and make things happen. Follow the phrase, *"Everything is fair in love and war."* Here you are in *love* with your success and fighting a *war* against failures. Ultimate aim is to achieve the goals. Once you succeed you are a winner – nothing less than that. I have never hesitated in accepting the challenges. Sometimes it sounded like gamble where 50% probability is that you win. But you should be smart enough to convert 50% failure also into success.

Also, try to avoid confrontation with the boss, but if you are left with Hobson's choice, then *take the bull by its horns* and move ahead. If you are clean, honest, and logical in approach, your trouble will be short-lived, and very soon you will make up for the loss. I did so. I remember a *doha* (two line poem) of an India Sant Kabir:

> *Jin khoja tin paiyan, gahare pani painth.*
> *Main bora duban dara, raha kinare baith.*

Meaning, thereby, whoever searched and made an attempt, sitting in the deep water (concentrating in risky conditions), achieved whatever was desired. I was scared of sinking and thus kept on sitting on the bank only.

Chapter 13
Temper Is Valuable Don't Lose It but Manage Anger

In the beginning of my service I had a two wheeler and naturally a helmet also which had a caption *Temper is Valuable Don't Lose it*, written on it. I found it to be so true. I guess all of us at one time or the other have shouted or raised our voices during the conversation. There are many reasons for the same like commanding a parade, asking for help, trying to draw attention, going through terrible pain or in the rage of anger etc. I will touch up on the rage of anger because this is more relevant to our subject while others depend on individual tolerance levels.

In my study, a person raises the voice for different reasons – one in the rage of anger where you can feel some metabolic changes taking place in your body – specially the arms while the other is to create scare to get the job done. First is harmful while the second is harmless. The bosses with first type of anger are vindictive and dangerous while those of second type are harmless and good at heart. There is third type where the angry person will become extra polite or even laugh when they are angry. They are the most dangerous. They are like silent heart attack and are masters in back stabbing. In one of the organization there was a very vindictive boss – Mr. Khanna (Not the real name). He was like a *boss* and not a *leader* and was never satisfied with the work of any subordinates. He used to express his unhappiness with someone by laughing a loud. His degree of unhappiness was directly proportional to the pitch of his laughter. In the office he was known as, "Happy Khanna." Employees used to avoid him unless there was no option. They used to say that going in front of "Happy Khanna" is worse than going behind a horse (If you are standing behind a horse, donkey, mule, giraffe or zebra, it will kick).

I have experienced that there is a tendency in the weak, incompetent and hollow supervisors to shout because they are scared of their failures and are incapable of handling situations which evolves in the organization because of someone's failure or lack of knowledge or carelessness. I have also seen that when they are shouting and the subordinate replies back their temper gets deflated immediately and they become polite. In my mind these are cunning people because after getting defeated they look for an opportunity to take revenge.

I have raised my voice only three times in my life time and non in the rage of anger. Two were on dishonesty and one was when someone commented adversely on my country in an international forum, but didn't harm them in their annual appraisal. I believe in:

Why should we harm our body by losing our temper for the mistake of others?

All said and done there are situations when sometimes you have to pull up someone to set the course right. If that be so there are certain rules which I recommend to follow. Firstly put yourself in his/her shoes before starting off. Before getting on the conversation be polite and get him/her acceptance of the *avoidable* carelessness. Once he/she does it, do the needful only in short and crisp communication. It will be effective otherwise the accuse will stop listening to you and may retaliate.

In doing so, I used to follow certain thumb rules. One – never be sarcastic. It has deep penetration. Two – never raise your voice in public or in front of juniors. It is very hurting and insulting. The people around, brand you an uncultured joker. It is good practice to praise publicly and pull up privately. Three – never pull up anyone when the person is having his/her main meals. It damages emotionally. We all work to earn for our meals. In the Indian Army the teaching is that when a person is having his/her meals he/she is not supposed to stand up even if the senior officer comes. Also no senior person is supposed to pull up the junior colleague on dining table. I fully endorse and follow the culture.

In order to avoid the failure of a task the onus of selection of right person and periodical monitoring of the progress rests on the supervisor who should evaluate the staff member's competence and availability for the job in advance. At the end if the staff member has done an acceptable job and you pat his back and say, "You have done an excellent job but improve on these aspects." Believe you me, next time he will put his heart and soul and give an excellent output. But on the contrary if the staff member has put his heart and soul and given you an output which is acceptable and your reaction is, "Oh my God you have not done anything. Simply wasted your time in producing this garbage." The staff member will get de-motivated and next time he/she will produce garbage only. I have seen both types of incidents.

Causes of anger are when you disagree with the other person because of any reason or someone disagrees with you with your thinking. The superior person tries to bulldoze you to make you agree with his point of view while you try to insist on your approach if you have clear conviction. Both of you raise voices and the complete office listens. In case it is a domestic quarrel, then neighbors have the feast and get juicy material for gossip mongering for the next day's coffee break. No one other than the persons involved can resolve the issue except making fun of the incidence. Ultimately the bone of contention settles down but it leaves an irremovable scar in the relations.

Anger Management is a full subject. Enterprising people are running training institutes for the same. Reason for getting angry is that you want the other person to be like you –think like you, behave like you and do everything like you while the other person also expects the same from you. No one but you only can control your state of anger. It can't be done with by switching a button but requires efforts to do so. I never get involved in argument with a person in the fit of anger. I feel pity on them as they are already torturing their body so I keep a cool and pleasing disposition and put counter reasons in a polite and soft manner. This way the angry persons get defused when they see no counter attack. After all they also have limited stamina to remain irritated.

*While in argument, improving the quality of your logic will have more penetrating effect,
rather than raising the pitch of your voice.*

Chapter 14
Offence and Punishment

All organizations have human resources to support the identical working of various departments. Laws, rules, guidelines, standard operating procedures etc exist, for systematic running of the same. However, managers at various levels are empowered to deviate from these policies in the best interest of the organization. They are known as Competent Authorities. Any action of deviation over shooting your authority without approval of Competent Authorities, from the laid down rules could be considered as commitment of offence. Depending on the gravity of offence disciplinary actions are required to be taken by the management. If it is felt that a person is guilty of offence first verbally investigate and if prima fascia it is established then proceed for further action immediately. The case should be decided expeditiously otherwise the productive time of the organization is wasted. I have never punished a person financially that is leading to reduction in pay and allowances. However, in the cases of physical damage to the property or intentional financial loss, the recovery was made.

I have never punished a person two times for the same offence. The aim of punishment has to be to reform the accuse and to set example for others in the organization. Never take any decision in anger. Also never award recordable punish to anyone without proper investigations.

Chapter 15
Training and Change Management

In the current century there is a revolution in every field. The world is changing at a super fast pace. The ways of doing business is rapidly taking unexpected turns. Redundancy is catching up over night. I feel it is attributed to very powerful human brain which is being exercised more and more in every walk of life and thus bringing out innovative ideas.

In order to keep up with dynamic pace it is necessary to continuously update yourself lest you are left behind. The employer doesn't hesitate to drop you from the team if you have obsolete knowledge. Therefore, training the professionals is another flourishing business and churns lot of funds. But to train others first you have to learn the new technology online or going to training institute. I have seen managers who are not good in practicing turn into preaching/ training/consulting. All countries have different culture and thus a tool which is successful in one country may not be useful in another country. What to say of different country but within the same country in a different geographical location because of cultural differences. I recommend that managers before selecting a tool must study the same in totality and suitability for their environment.

For example, in the 1980's the Japanese methods were very much talked about in manufacturing industry. One of them was "Just in time," commonly known as JIT in inventory management. In this method the outsourced items used in making the end product were to be brought just in time when they were required in the assembly line and not kept in stores in advance to reduce the inventory holding cost. In developed countries it was possible but not in all the developing countries. Top management insisted in following JIT but very soon every one realized that it is not that easy. I leave it to you to visualize the problems in your experience – transport, traffic, labor problems, strikes, shortage of raw material etc. JIT quite often used to make manufacturing team jittery.

I will not emphasis further on the continuous training and logical implementation of new tools for overall change management.

Chapter 16
Terms of Reference (ToR) of the Jobs and Standard Operating Procedures (SOP)

In order to have systematic working of the operations it is important to have laid down Terms of Reference for various job/appointments with responsibilities/accountability, powers and hierarchy clearly defined. The same should be handed over to the new employees and explained clearly.

Similarly it is a good practice to have exhaustive SOP for all operations and keep them updated. Need based incorporation of amendments should be a dynamic process.

Chapter 17
Under Cutting and Cockroach/Crab Mentality

If you are a rising star because of qualities and smartness, you are an eye sour in the eyes of your peers. They keep looking for opportunity for giving you an under cut. It is very important that you are always alert to guard yourself against such attempts. People who can't compete with you professionally, try to do back biting and do the actions to sabotage your execution of plans to bring you down in the eyes of the supervisors. Be cautious of extra sweet colleagues at work place. Remember the famous story of *cockroach/crab mentality*. Keep doing the good work with both your eyes and ears open.

Once I had accepted the challenge of turning around a sick organization. Everyone in the head office (HO) was hell bent to create hurdles in my efforts. While I was implementing my plans to make the organization profitable, people in HO were leaving no stone unturned in their attempts to let me down. In 1980s cordless phones were new and to have the same in the office used to give higher managers a sense of superiority and pride without realizing that the cordless phones used to work on Amplitude

Modulation (AM) technology which could be received on a normal hand held AM transistor. One day in the evening I tuned my transistor on and was shocked to hear conversation between two senior persons of the organization talking against me. I heard their complete conversation and next day I confronted them reproducing full details of their conversation. They were speechless. It raised alarm for me and I became extra cautious and reduced sharing my turn around plans in informal talks.

Chapter 18
Variety of People in Organization

In any organization you come across variety of people working under you – multicultural, multinational, different religion, multi region, multi gender, multi ages, multi temperament, multi ego etc. In nutshell no two persons are same. You have to handle them individually on their personalities. I observed that in India people who belong to one region don't conversate without using abusive language in every sentence. A person who is talking to them and doesn't use abuses freely is considered odd. On the other hand the persons with another region are so sensitive that if someone talks to them even in loud tone, they pull a long face.

It is therefore, very important that as manager you should have an adequate if not thorough knowledge of customs and behavior of variety of people under you. Always appreciate and respect their feelings and never utter a single word which turns out to be derogatory to their feelings. This situation becomes more challenging when operating in multinational culture.

Chapter 19
Participative Management (Quality Circles)

During my time of working at various levels of seniority I tried and successfully practiced the method of participative management. In 1980s there was a fashion of implementing a management tool called Quality Circles (QC). I found it to be an ideal example of participative management. Unfortunately, it got faded out over the period when the fashion changed in the style of management.

A small introduction of QC for those who are not aware of it. After the World War II the utilization of QC in Japan had been largely responsible for rebuilding the shattered economy. It can be defined as:

Quality Circle is a small group of employees – generally less than 10, in the same work area or doing similar nature of work, voluntarily meet on a required frequency to identify, analyze and resolve work related problems leading to improve and make existing process simpler and economical.

The small groups are one for each problem. Once the problem is resolved the actions are documented and group is closed. I found it very interesting tool and used it in all areas of operations successfully including with the players to make the winning strategy in tournaments. It works even in family discussions to handle the domestic issues. The best part is that in QC the persons who are on ground and are aware of all the aspects of the situation put their heads together and take out the solution. This gives them a sense of immense job satisfaction and they feel proud of their contribution to the organization. Many a times these QC recommendations have resulted into financial gain in the costing of the product. Such Circles are applauded and rewarded.

These recommendations may look small but lead to big gains hence should be given full importance.

Chapter 20
Delegation and Empowerment

Many of the bosses don't believe in delegating their authorities to the subordinates and empower them to take the decisions because of lack of mutual confidence. This makes everyone to run to them even for the smallest decisions. These are the people who are the bottlenecks in smooth running of the systems because of late decisions and have no time for their constructive thinking. Even more important is that the capable persons under them feel totally frustrated and the atmosphere of work place is spoilt. Never hesitate in delegating and empowering the subordinates. But while doing so suitability and availability of the selected person is to be ensured. Also initially he/she is to be closely monitored to guard against damaging surprises till you have developed full confidence in him/her.

Although it is a good management practice to delegate and empower the suitable employees for taking decisions but the overall responsibility of failsafe functioning rests on your shoulders only. One of the HoD under me in his morning briefing reported slow progress in his task. When I asked him the reason he replied, "Sir you had asked HoDs to delegate and empower the junior staff so I delegated this job to Mr. Slow Speed. He has not completed it. What can I do?" I replied to him, "Mr. HoD, you registered my half instructions. I had advised everyone to delegate but you can't shirk your overall responsibility of being HoD. How you monitor Mr. Slow Speed, is your prerogative and skill. In case you are not sure how to do it you can consult with anyone including me because we all are in a team and help each other." No harm could be done because it was my *work in progress* monitoring.

Chapter 21
Circulate Grapevine Before Passing Sensitive Orders

As managers you have to take decisions affecting all persons working under you. Generally all decisions are taken with good intentions which are beneficial to all but sometimes hard decisions are not accepted kindly. In such situations I used to spread the grapevine and closely observe the air. Based on the reaction of masses I used to either modify the actions or if required discuss the same in Town Hall Meeting. It worked very well.

Chapter 22
Extra Marital Relations or Stealing the Affection of Colleague's Spouse

In today's work environment it is very common that men and women work very closely in the organizations/projects for long time, sometimes may be for extended hours and become good friends. If you feel that you are crossing the barrier of friendship and coming closer to your team mate immediately control your emotions especially if one of you is married. This phenomenon is known as, *"Stealing the love and affection of colleague's spouse."* Extra marital relations, generally, lead you to mental tension and poor performance at work place and at home.

But if both of you are unmarried then there should be no problem.

Chapter 23
Avoid Roadside Brawls

Road rages and brawls are increasing every day. You also unintentionally get involved in argument with the other professional driver thus equating yourself to him. I feel when you sit on the driver's seat you also start behaving like one and forgetting your social status of manager you tend to equate with him and thus get into a brawl with him. In such situations keep yourself above than the thinking of a driver and handle the situation gracefully and remains calm in crisis. The brawls are because people are hassled in daily life, distances are long, competition of earning more and more is getting hotter etc. Thus they are all charged up. Slightest argument leads to spark the fuel of intolerance. They don't realize the aftermath of incidence. Too many legal hassles.

In some places if the accident takes place both the parties call the insurance companies who take care of the repairs. The drivers shake hands and smile before parting. I like this way of resolving, as accident is accident and not done intentionally.

Chapter 24
Eye for Details

As manager you should keep your eyes and ears open always and ever. Do your work with full concentration so that it is "Right the first time (RFT)." All out effort should be done to avoid rework. In your training sessions always insist on RFT. Rework is de-motivating, de-moralizing and time consuming.

Chapter 25
Self Grooming and Etiquettes

On reaching the managerial cadre you are definitely going to be involved in various international travels, meeting senior and interacting with well placed people. If you are not matching with the manners and etiquettes required in that society you will feel lacking behind and hesitate to communicate with them. A properly well dressed person with sharp disposition impresses everyone at the first sight. Besides, your immaculate table manners add to the overall personality. A manager should be able to impress the gathering and should not be behaving in cheap and disgusting manner.

If you feel that you are not meeting the expected level, please don't hesitate in taking a training course on grooming. It is not embarrassing.

Chapter 26
Social Activities

Human beings are social animals. Having regular social get together with the friends, you and spouse get along, rejuvenates you. I have a No. of social circles of likeminded people (LMP) that is why even after retirement we don't get bored and have at least two social events to attend per week. My circles are those of school and engineering college friends, army friends, UN friends, selected relatives etc.

Besides this we have membership of two clubs – one in Delhi and another in NOIDA. We organize two formal parties to celebrate our wedding anniversary and my birthday (My wife's birthday and our wedding anniversary is on the same day, hence two parties.). After that we keep getting invitations throughout the year. Small parties with limited No. of friends are ongoing activities. So throughout the year there are no dull moments.

My wife and I are fond of a lot of reading on new happenings around the globe and for that we depend on both print and electronic media. We believe in the saying:

The Best book is equal to hundred good friends,
But one excellent friend is equal to a library.

Case Studies

Chapter 27
Not Getting Along in Joint Families

Two generations living in joint family after marriage not getting along is a global phenomenon. Generally mother and sister get together and try to ridicule the daughter-in-law who has joined the family. They don't realize that a lady who has left her home to make your son's home should be supported to get adjusted smoothly. The daughter-in-law sees both the other ladies as potential threat to her process of peacefully settling down. She has her dreams of how to make her family with her husband. The husband who has been in the focus of mother and sister starts sharing his attention with his wife which is natural and there is nothing wrong in doing so. One of the big reasons is love marriage against the parents' approval. This subject is so big that a separate book can be written on it.

I had a newly wedded lady Sugandha (Name changed) working in software organization under me as developer. She used to stay with her in-laws in the same house on the first floor. Theirs was a love marriage. Her husband was also doing well in the Sales and Marketing field. Her mother-in-law was a senior government officer. I expected her mother-in-law being a working woman to be more liberal and accommodative but unfortunately she was not. Nagging between the two ladies was a daily ritual on flimsy non-issues. Sugandha and her husband were not at all at ease. One day she told me her domestic problem. I advised her to call her husband also for meeting. He came and we discussed various possibilities at length in totality and reached to the conclusion that they should step out of the house and start living in separate flat close by so that they are not interacting with interfering parent everyday and yet are not far away to attend to them in case of emergency.

They did it and found the relations improved. Later I was told that as anticipated the parents went to Sugandha's house and patched up to stay together. This advice I give to all young couples including my children to stay away from parents at least for a couple of years till the newlyweds also understand each other and don't wait for differences to grow with in-laws and then separate.

Lesson learnt: It is advisable for newly wedded couples not to stay in joint families for a couple of years because everyone wants to make their own dream home. The couple has to understand each other make joint decisions to live as they plan. It is not possible in a joint family even if you stay on a separate floor. This is the reason when children stay in different cities the bonding among them and also with in-laws is better and stronger.

Chapter 28
Sacking an Engineer on Dishonesty

My organization was developing an Electronic Push Button Telephone for Post Telegraph and Telephone Department (In India known as Bharat Sanchar Nigam Limited – BSNL). I had selected a young engineer to work in the team as quality assurance person and also liaise with BSNL engineers. He was very smart and technically very sound to the extent that he became almost indispensible person in the project. His job responsibility involved fair amount of travelling.

Once he returned from a tour and submitted the bills of his expenditure. The Finance Manager observed that this engineer had over written on the bills increasing the actual expenditure. It was done very clearly and boldly which showed his innocence. When the case was brought to me I called him and asked him the reason for doing so. He honestly told me that he has done the dishonesty because he wanted to make extra money. Normally the wheeler dealers do such activities in a smarter way and never get caught. But this guy was naïve and was caught.

He was an asset to our organization but as Head I couldn't have tolerate the dishonesty. So I sacked him immediately to set example for others too.

Lesson learnt: Dishonesty at work place is not to be tolerated as this sets bad precedence which is invariably misquoted.

Chapter 29
Punishment Reforms

While I was a young officer in Indian army I had a soldier Tiwari (name changed) under me. He was intelligent and smart but very lazy and shammer. He was supposed to clear certain promotion examinations which he was deliberately avoiding and hence his promotion was getting delayed. In army it is the responsibility of the superior officer to ensure that their subordinates don't lose promotions for not being qualified. I asked his supervisor why Tiwari is not clearing the examinations. Supervisor told me that he is not interested is promotion. I punished him for this reason which was allowed under the Military Law. After getting the punishment, I came to know that Tewari had suddenly become very serious in studies and had cleared all the promotions examinations step by step. Time passed and I bumped into him again after six years in a different duty station. He was a Junior Commissioned Officer (Class II Gazetted Officer in Army) after clearing all his mandatory examinations at a fast pace. He came to me, smartly saluted and said, "Sir if you would not have punished me to make me realize my mistake, I would have retired as soldier only with meager pension. But I am a JCO now and because of my excellent performance I am likely to retire as honorary officer with multifold pension and respect in my village."

Lesson learnt: Punishment reforms too. But while awarding the punishment and later the supervisors should continuously counsel the person for his mistakes. That is why in good old days the jails were known as Reformatories.

Chapter 30
Never Promote Incompetent Person

You must have heard a story of a king and the monkey. In short it goes like this. There was a very powerful king. He was a keen hunter of tigers. One day he went in jungle and since he was tired he went to sleep under a tree. Suddenly a tiger came with an intention to kill the king. A monkey sitting on the tree saw it and started making alarming noises. The king got up and killed the tiger. King was very happy with monkey. Then onwards, monkey used to accompany king in all his hunting sprees.

While on hunting one day king was tired and he told the monkey to be cautious so that nobody disturbs him in the sleep. Monkey accepted the responsibility. King went to sleep. One fly came around the king and sat on his nose. Monkey didn't like it. He took out king's sword and attacked on fly. It flew away but monkey chopped off King's nose, instead. I have seen in my experience that promoters *(king)* for the reasons best known to them hire incompetent professionals who bring bad name to organizations.

I remember a case where in the promoter *(king)* happen to meet a senior professional *Mr. Dipper, the monkey* during the meeting of Confederation of Industries and got impressed. *Mr. Dipper* was hired as the Director of the company which was growing at a good pace with old loyalists sitting on the driving seats. *Mr. Dipper* came with an idea of revolutionizing the establishment's working. Where ever he went he condemned the processes and systems of star performing company which in the previous year had outshined all the production units in India and was given national award for the quality product. He started bullying the HoDs for non performance and came up with the weird ideas to promote the business. But within one year of his arrival the profit graph started dipping. In the second year *Mr. Dipper, the monkey* brought bad name *(Chopped the nose)* to an excellent organization and the king had to sack him.

Lesson learnt: Never hire/promote *monkeys* in the organizations otherwise they will chop your nose off. And also if you will give peanuts as remunerations to the employees, you will get such monkeys only.

Chapter 31
Provide Necessary Facilities

I was new to the organization where in I was hired with a clear mandate to turn the company around which had been making losses for over seven years. I always believe that if the manpower is well looked after and are contended they put in their best and the results are visible. One day while on a routine round of the assembly area I noticed that one women worker was looking very sad unlike her usual appearance. I asked her the reason which she replied, "I have a year old son. When I was preparing to leave for works he had high fever and was crying. I am thinking about him only." I thought this in one of the cases which has come to my notice, there could be more. I called the Manager Administration and instructed him to make a Crèche for the small babies with all facilities. It was done. We had a Crèche in factory which was patronized by 16 women employees. The result was that the absenteeism of women employees got reduced.

Lesson learnt: At the work place try to give maximum facilities to employees which eases their stresses and help in increasing the productivity.

Chapter 32
Regularize the Actions Beyond Control

The incident goes back to 1980s. I was commanding an army unit. There was no arrangement of hot water for the soldiers for taking bath. I thought of providing the same for two reasons one it was a welfare measure for the troops and secondly I decided to use solar panels for the purpose to educate soldiers about the new technology which they could promote in their villages too. There was no running expenditure of power consumption after the initial investment which was subsidized by the government. Also the use of non conventional energy was in fashion too. I got lots of appreciation in the military station for this initiative.

But I did the mistake of keeping its hot water tap outside in open. In winters when the hot water was available soldiers started having bath in open leading to stagnation of water near living area. I neither wanted to let this happen nor deprive the soldiers of hot water. The orders were to collect hot water in buckets and go to the bath room. Despite my continuous advice they didn't stop taking bath near the tap. This was not an offence where harsh disciplinary action was required.

So I got a proper Bathing Point made duly decorated with tiles and towel rails. This was officially declared as Hot Water Bathing Point – an additional welfare activity. The outlet was connected with proper drains to dispense with water stagnation and breeding of mosquitoes.

Lesson learnt: Never be rigid if your flexible approach could facilitate the system without violating the rule of the land.

Chapter 33
Determination of Joining Army and United Nations

During my engineering college days I saw an advertisement for the position of Naval Fighter pilot. I found that I was qualified and applied for the position. I was surprised when I got a call to appear for Pilot Aptitude Battery Test (PABT). Since I was already doing engineering degree every one advised me against it but I thought if I get selected I will have more self confidence. On reaching the Selection Board I noticed there were three batches of 50 candidates each. We were made to take PABT on a simulator. The Air Force Officers who were conducting it told everyone that this test is given only once in the life time. I was not under stress because I had gone there to gain some experience. The test was completed and out of 150 candidates I was the only one who qualified. At the age of 17+ years I had crossed first test. This was followed by Services Selection Board (SSB) Interview for assessing Officer Like Qualities (OLQ). It lasted for three days followed by medical test. I cleared all. This made me confident that after passing out from engineering college no one can stop me from joining army as a President Commissioned Officer.

There was a great recession in the market when our batch passed out. Students were accepting intern jobs. I appeared in SSB and cleared it because of my previous exposure but was rejected in the medical test. I appealed against the decision and was asked to reappear for medical examination at Command Hospital who cleared me without any hic ups. I joined army as commissioned officer at the age of 21+ years. I think it was because of my determination that I succeeded in my attempts.

Later after taking premature retirement I thought of joining United Nations to attain global exposure. It took me a while. I applied for 350+ posts in Peace Keeping Operations in five years and then I got one which changed my life altogether.

Lesson learnt: If you are determined to do something never give in. Ultimately the success will be in your feet.

Chapter 34
Remain Cool in Crisis

While in crisis if you remain cool you think logically and handle the situation without getting confused. I was going to office in my car. When my driver saw a green signal on the traffic light he brought the car in motion. But suddenly one three wheeler auto rickshaw came jumping the red signal and hit the fanner of my car from a right angle. My car got dents and the bumper came out but his auto rickshaw lost the balance and toppled. He was carrying some small primary level students to school. They were scattered on the road and because of fear they started crying. The driver also fell down and had minor bruises. I checked each and every child; luckily no one even had any bruise. I made them cool down and sent them off to their school. By now a crowd of about 100 persons got together and encircled me and started shouting slogans against me. I climbed on a slightly higher platform with an intention to see all of them while addressing. I called the driver of the auto rickshaw also to stand with me.

I asked him, "Why were you driving fast and why did you jump the red traffic light?" He replied in front of all the gathered crowd, "Today is my festival and I don't have money to celebrate it. My children are at home waiting for me. I was rushing thinking that after leaving the students in the school, I will drop some passengers and collect money for celebration." He was in a pitiable condition. His auto rickshaw super structure was also smashed. I thought poverty is very bad in any ones' life. On humanitarian ground I gave him adequate cash for stitch repair of his vehicle and celebration of the festival. He started crying with folded hands in front of me while the crowd started clapping. I felt very satisfied internally and proceeded to my office

Lesson learnt: Remain cool in crisis and take actions after quickly analyzing the situation. But always be humanitarian.

Chapter 35
Aiming for Perfection

In the ideal situation it is recommended to be perfect in all walks of life but it is not possible to do so practically. Perfection means 100% but in reality if you can achieve six sigma level, it is as good as perfection. Positive exponential curve in the performance will take you to "tending to perfection" but not cent percent. So don't sweat for ideal results as you will never have ideal situations in operations.

While teaching perfection I narrate this self made story – a satire, of a battle to the audience. In one of the operations the headquarters (HQ) had given a task to lower formation to capture a location. The Commander at HQ called the Team Leader and explained him the situation and task along with the time frame on a sand model and map. The team Leader understood the aim. As a practice it was now the duty of the Staff Officer (SO) in the HQ to release operation orders. The team Leader when asked SO, he responded, "Sir, it will take another 30 minutes as the clerk who typed (those days mechanical typewriters were in use) the Op Order has done some punctuation and spelling mistakes. I did not like the quality of document." Team leader replied, "I am not worried about icing so long the cake is available. I have understood the complete plan and I am itching to proceed." The time of departure was fixed as 1800 hrs. Team leader had not received the Op Order till then, so he decided to leave as per plan without them. The team accomplished the mission on time and gave a completion report to HQ. Everybody congratulated the Team Leader. SO after greeting also said, "Sir, Op Orders are ready. There are no typing mistakes in it."

Lesson learnt: It is good to be perfect but not at the cost of some other risk.

Conclusion

I have summarized my real-life experiences in a simple language and avoided making it a heavy reading. I have experienced that smart work; quick, flexible and accurate decisions help you succeed in totality in life. Remain cool during the crisis and neither compare yourself with anyone nor try blindly to follow others. This will help you to think rationally. Look after the human resource that you lead and listen to their suggestions. Have back up plans so that business continues as usual. Focused and determined approach will make you come out with flying colors in all your endeavors.

www.ingramcontent.com/pod-product-compliance
Lightning Source LLC
Chambersburg PA
CBHW030855180526
45163CB00004B/1585